C000270335

Welcome to "Liverpool Then", the first in a special collection of heritage specials celebrating Merseyside life past and present. We've created a remarkable photographic collection for you to keep, using some of the finest images from the archives of the Liverpool Echo and Daily Post.

Why not contribute your own historic Merseyside photographs and memories to share with others over the internet, using our online People's Archive?
This special feature aims to establish a gallery of pictures and memories of life in our region.
It can be accessed by visiting the websites for the Daily Post (www.liverpooldailypost.co.uk)
or Liverpool Echo (www.liverpoolecho.co.uk) and clicking on the People's Archive icon.

Alternatively, if any of the images in "Liverpool Then" spark a personal recollection, or you want to write and tell us about old Liverpool and submit pictures for future use, simply write to: "Liverpool Then", PO Box 48, Old Hall Street, Liverpool L69 3EB. Remember to include your own name and address.

The newly restored photographs featured in this book, plus other pictures from the Liverpool Daily Post and Echo archives, are available to buy.
Simply visit www.merseyshop.com/photos or telephone 0151 472 2549 (Monday to Friday 10am to 4pm)

Above Gwladys Street residents celebrate the 1953 Coronation in the shadow of Goodison Park

Sitting, unmoved
and unmoving,

staring through the window,
with glazed expression.

Your life in neutral
while the earth
rotates around you.

At least it gives you
time to dream,

of not being in traffic.

Top   Morris dancing policemen change places on point duty in Everton Valley in 1963
Above Convoys of green buses dominated the Lime Street scene in the early Sixties

The opening of Knowsley Safari Park. A Mark 1 Cortina leads the snaking river of cars waiting patiently to have their windscreen wipers attacked by monkeys in July 1971. And all for the princely sum of £1 per car

On a scorching Sunday in June 1967, that quick trip up the coast to Southport seemed like a good idea at the time

Farewell to the trams. A procession of Baby Grands on the last trip to Bowring Park on September 14, 1957

Top Balaclava, wellies, jacket held together with a safety pin and a Saturday afternoon treat feeding the pigeons at the Pier Head. The good old days...
Above Children perform "The Land of Everywhere" on Exchange Flags as part of the city's celebrations for the Silver Jubilee of King George V in 1935

People then

were just like people now,

but poorer

and thinner,

with less fashion sense

Top   City diners join high society with the opening of the Tower Restaurant on St John's Beacon in 1971
Above Groovy baby! The opening night of the Adelphi Hotel's disco in January 1972

Walk across town today.

All those euromillions
and tons of concrete.

Is it an interesting place any more?

or are we sleepwalking into

Retail-on-Sea?

Top The original July 1950 caption for this photograph says it all:
"In less than five hours the road surface of Moorfields, which links
Dale Street and Tithebarn Street, was re-covered yesterday by five men"

Above Time for a chat in the cloisters of the Dockers' Umbrella, beneath the
Overhead Railway's Pier Head Station

Lord Street and Church Street on a damp September day in 1957

As the Sixties turned to the Seventies, the docks around the Pier Head were still in use and the redevelopment of the city waterfront was just beginning

A grey November day on Old Hall Street in 1976. The lights blaze in the
Cotton Exchange as a crane rises above the skeleton of Ralli House

A Dingle-bound train pulls into James Street Overhead Railway station in 1935

Top Demolition of the Overhead Railway's Pier Head station in 1957
Above Delivery lorries block Temple Court alongside the Fruit Exchange on Victoria Street in 1962

Does anyone miss

waking up to ice on the inside
of the bedroom window?

Thank God for double glazing

and central heating.

Top Heavy September rains brought floods to Prescot Road in 1955
Above Spectators wait in vain for a break in the weather during a professional
tennis tournament at Liverpool Cricket Club in 1958

Calderstones Park becomes a winter wonderland for two boys and a sledge in February 1958

The camera captures the full force of this 1956 blizzard as it sweeps across cars parked on St George's Plateau

She ain't heavy, she's my neighbour. Flash floods following a summer storm in July 1965 bring chaos to Great Nelson Street

Workmen in Sefton Park carry warning notices down to the lake in 1961

Top Braving the lunchtime elements along Lime Street in December 1964
Above Ignoring the aftermath of an August thunderstorm in 1959, a train clangs its way past Cunard Building along the Liverpool Dock Estate railway line

Sand in your butties,

a bucketful of cockles on
the train coming home from
New Brighton.

Sunburn on your neck,

sleeping on the Crosville
coming home from Wales.

Top   Welcome shade for young picnickers in Bowring Park on a hot summer's day in the 1920s
Above After long years of war, a sunny August day at New Brighton Baths comes as welcome relief in 1945

It's 6.15pm on a hot June day in 1960 and the long trek home begins

Top August temperatures in the high 80s brought the crowds to Wirral's Meols Slipway in 1955
Above In 1955 the Isle of Man had 584,528 summer visitors, a fair percentage of them waiting for the Manx boats on this July morning

City centre workers soak up the lunchtime sunshine in Coronation Gardens in 1957

Top "As long as I gaze on Wavertree sunset, I am in paradise"
Above Fun in the sun for mums and toddlers at Stanley Park paddling pool in June 1961

Love is in the air... at New Brighton

Easter Sunday crowds at Hoylake in 1947 enjoy the sun, but one man has brought his overcoat, just in case

More listed buildings than other city apart from London.

More Georgian houses than Bath.
We wear our great buildings like fine clothes,
the tailored elegance of a wardrobe of Savile Row suits.

Each a perfect fit. A statement of confidence and style.

Some, frayed at the edges, in need of restoration.

All deserving of our love and care.

Top   The facade of the original St John's Market building, which was demolished in 1964. Only the Liver Bird finial above the entrance was saved
Above In 1941 the great escape from the drabness and menace of war was in cinemas like the Forum in Lime Street.
This is April 1941, a week before the onslaught of the May Blitz

Looking up William Brown Street and Islington from Dale Street in 1951, with St Francis Xavier's Church on the skyline

Renshaw Street, 1941. The Central Hall of the Liverpool Methodist Mission opened in 1905

Firemen damp down a fire in the Queen Anne South Wing of Croxteth Hall, home of Lord Sefton.
The blaze in December 1952 would have been much worse but for the prompt action of the French chef, Raymond Lempereurs

St George's Crescent in 1907, which was built on the site of Liverpool Castle Ditch. It formed part of the perimeter of St George's Church, which itself was on the site of the present Victoria Monument

Folklore has it that the female Liver Bird faces the sea waiting for her lover's return, while the male bird on the East Tower faces the city to see if the pubs are open

Bunney's, once Liverpool's most handsome store, seen here in 1956 the year it was sold to Greenwoods. Tragically this magnificent building at the junction of Church Street and Whitechapel was lost in 1957 when the corner was redeveloped

Central Station and Ranelagh Street as seen from the roof of Lewis's in 1957

Coopers' Church Street store showing Church Lane, which disappeared when C&A expanded in the Seventies.
The iconic food store ground its last coffee bean on March 11, 1972

One of the city's most fondly remembered landmarks, the Guinness Clock on the Imperial Hotel, Lime Street

Top   Codman's Punch and Judy in its original site, The Quadrant, Lime Street in 1957
Above Post-war entertainment for children of all ages in 1946

That's the way to do it!

Top The audience watches, fascinated
Above Professor Richard Codman contemplates the 1957 move from The Quadrant, home to Punch and Judy since 1860, to St George's Plateau

Final preparations for the official opening of the Queensway Tunnel in July 1934

"We built the
Mersey Tunnel, boys

Way back in 'thirty-three

Dug an 'ole in the ground
until we found

An 'ole called Wallasey,

And the foreman cried,
Come on outside

the roof is falling down

And I'm tellin' you Jack,
we all swam back

To dear old
Liverpool town."

I wish I was back in Liverpool
by Stan Kelly-Bootle

Top King George V and Queen Mary open the Queensway Tunnel on July 18, 1934
Above A cavalcade of coaches are checked for height clearance to avoid the contractor's gear
before the official Queensway opening. Many of them had to have their tyres deflated

The Old Haymarket disappears to make way for the Queensway Tunnel entrance

"It is the boast
of Liverpool

that the horses employed
in the city's industry
are the finest in the kingdom,

and it is a boast to which
it is scarcely possible
to take exception."

Quote from a 1914 guidebook to Liverpool

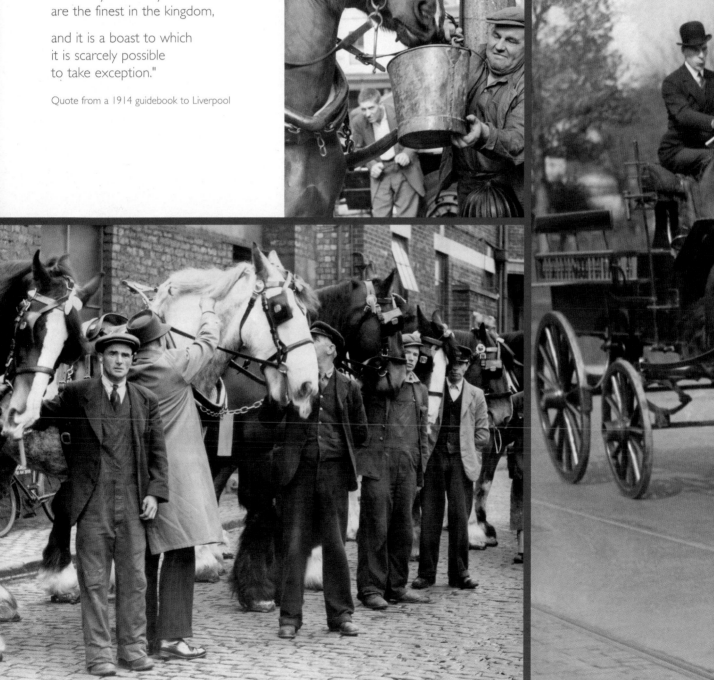

Top   Elevenses for the binman's horse in 1959
Above Inspection time for the horses from British Railway's Park Lane Goods Station in June 1948

Tuition for the newly appointed coachman to the Lord Mayor, as he takes a four-in-hand brake through Sefton Park in 1937

Only the Playhouse and the corner of the John Lewis store can be recognised from this view of Williamson Square in 1956

Cooling off in the Steble Fountain on William Brown Street

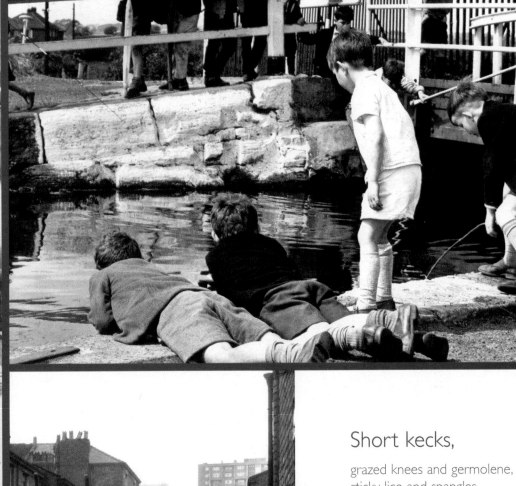

Short kecks,

grazed knees and germolene,
sticky lice and spangles,
playing footy in the dark...
a liverpool kid

what's the time mister wolf?
time for bed yer mam says,
wash yer face, say yer prayers
and dream of playing footy in the park...
a liverpool kid

long kecks, spotty face and clearasil,
beech-nut and woodbines,
restless dreams of kissing her,
in the park, in the dark...
a liverpool kid

Top   Youngsters stop by the Leeds-Liverpool Canal on the way home from school in 1965
Above Three amigos, nothing but adventure lies ahead

It was thirsty work playing in Sefton Park. It's a good job Charles P Melly introduced Britain's first public drinking fountain in 1854. It was at Prince's Dock and was designed to keep dry-throated dockers out of the pub

It's just not fair... one little lad against all those girls!

The Belmont one of Liverpool's lost theatreland pubs, a quick dart from the Playhouse stage door in Houghton Street.
The last pint was pulled in 1964. Landlord Peter Callan serves a table of Playhouse regulars, including John Slater and Patrick Stewart

"I'll meet you in the...

A 1 at Lloyds, Australian Vaults,
Bear's Paw, Bleak House, Blue Ball,
Bodega, Caradoc, Cattle Market,
Court House, Cunard, Dart,
Duke's Crown, Flying Dutchman,
Greenland, Griffin, Huskisson,
Jamaica, Legs of Man, Liver Vaults,
Magic Clock, New Court,
Newington, North Star,
Old Spanish Wine House, Paganini,
Pie Shoppe, Queen of Diamonds,
Soho, Trawler, Trojan's Head,
Triton, Why Not."

Top The doyen of Liverpool licensees, Danny English of the Old Dive, one of the thirteen pubs that disappeared to make way for the new St John's Market development in 1964. Danny, assisted by the legendary Sadie behind the bar (the original Sexy Sadie), often played host to afternoon drinking sessions for the Beatles and other bands who played lunchtime sessions at the Cavern. In those days the pubs were closed between 3pm and 5pm

Above Mary Ellen Egerton was born in Ireland in 1863 and lived in London before taking over the American Bar on Lime Street. Following the demolition of the American Bar she moved to the Eagle Hotel in Pudsey Street behind the Empire Theatre. She counted Marie Lloyd and Charlie Chaplin among her many showbusiness friends. Today the pub bears her name, Ma Egerton's

Not the squire popping in for a snifter in some rural backwater, but the Childwall Abbey Hotel in 1947

Ma Boyle's Oyster Bar in its original location on Old Hall Street before the move to Tower Gardens in 1973. The old bar, which saw millions of pounds worth of cotton business taking place over lunch, had the famous sign "Gentlemen are requested not to smoke before 2.30pm"

You just had to be there!

Top The 1954 Orange Lodge procession makes its way up Moorfields to Exchange Station
Above Liverpool's own Speakers' Corner – free speech at the Pier Head in 1968

The Shaftesbury Memorial Fountain and Eros is unveiled in 1932. The Sefton Park Eros is a second casting of the figure which stands in Piccadilly Circus

'Vorsprung durch technik' (progress through technology), the Graf Zepellin,
soars over the Dock Road and Overhead Railway in 1932

Roseberry Street residents celebrate winning first prize in Liverpool's Charter Street Decorations Competition in 1957.
John Lennon and The Quarrymen played one of their first gigs from the back of a coal lorry as part of the street's celebrations

The Sixties, when everyone 'knew' the Beatles. Not too many Gibsons or Fenders on show in this array of Merseybeat hopefuls,
but plenty of Framus, Hofner and Futurama guitars bought on the drip from Hessy's. Appropriately in the middle of it all is Rory Storm,
one of the central characters in that vibrant decade

Top   Rock around the dock. Frankie Goes To Hollywood at the Albert Dock in 1986
Above Sefton Park, August Bank Holiday 1982. Echo And The Bunnymen kick off the Larks in the Park

Top   Celebrating our rural roots, the Liverpool and District Sheepdog Society trials are held at Greenhill Road in 1947

Above Liverpool Stadium hosts a crowd of 3,000 for a 1953 Coronation concert given by the Philharmonic Orchestra, Choir and Welsh Choral Union

A show of hands at a demonstration by the unemployed outside St George's Hall in 1921. Among the resolutions passed that day was free admittance to cinemas, theatres and music halls. One clergyman speaker proposed a 24-hour boycott of public houses. This was carried with cries of "We've got no money anyway"

An afternoon stroll with the kids down Church Lane alongside Walton Church

Where you belong,

where you walked
with your Mam and Dad,

where you knew
every crack in the pavement,

where you learned to ride a bike,

where you knew your neighbours,

where passers-by smiled,

where you go back to,

alone,

to remind yourself

Where you belong.

Top   Bustling Great Homer Street in 1958
Above Chorley Chambers at the Junction of Dale Street and Fontenoy Street in 1932,
          prior to its demolition

What better place to catch the late summer sun in 1964?

Residents in Lionel Street off Seymour Street, one of the city's pre-war slum clearance areas, in 1931

New tenements (**left**) being constructed on Byrom Street in 1938, replacing the old slums (**right**)

Roll out the barrel. Once one of the city's great trades, an apprentice is accepted as a fully fledged journeyman cooper by being rolled in a barrel along with pitch, shavings and dirty water

Today is your first day

Today you become an adult.
Today you go upstairs on the bus

where drifts of smoke
fromPlayers, Capstan and Seniors

embrace the steam
from thirty wet macks.

Today you paid full fare.

Today is your first day.

Today you are starting work.

Top   A labour of love. High above the city, the steelwork for the roof of the Metropolitan Cathedral is laid down
Above Buying the Echo on the way home, one of the rituals of the working day

Top Shoes and buttons shining, these call boys at the Cotton Exchange in 1954 get their orders for the day from the commissionaire
Above Buying, selling, lifting, carrying, pushing, pulling – all part of a day's work at the Fruit Market in Cazneau Street in 1969

Robbed of the dignity of work, the unemployed queue for food parcels from the Liverpool Echo Goodfellow Fund in 1935

Top Famous with seafarers across the globe, the second hand clothes stalls on Paddy's Market, seen in 1957
Above 1952 brought a change in the law, giving pedestrians the right of way across zebra crossings and one over-zealous errand boy feels the full weight of the law

No hypermarkets
or supermarkets,

just markets

No designer shops,

just shops.

No internet shopping,

just boys on bikes.

Top and above   Daly's family tobacconists on Scotland Road first opened its doors in 1897. Started by Irish immigrant James Daly,
it lay at the heart of the Irish community. The business finally closed down in 1983, marking the end of an era.
At the time of its closure the shop was still selling Irish newspapers

"We'll miss

the Mary Ellens,
and me Dad'll miss the docks,

An Gran'll miss the washouse
where she washed
me Grandad's socks.

Don't want to go to Kirkby,
or Skelmersdale or Speke,

Don't want to go from all we
know in Back Buchanan Street."

Back Buchanan Street
by Harry and Gordon Dison

Top Once the beating heart of the Scotland Road community, in the Sixties slum clearance made the area behind St Anthony's Church a wasteland
Above Looking down Havelock Street towards Seacombe Towers in 1968.
As the terraces along Everton Valley fall, new homes rise in the sky in their place

Former residents of Caernarvon Street watch their homes being demolished in 1962

Looking from Brunswick Road across the city in 1973. Memories, turned to dust, are carried away on the breeze

Over a hundred people queued for the chance to rent this two-up-two-down in Ono Street, Wavertree, in September 1960. In spite of the upstairs damp and lack of hot water there were no shortage of takers, even with the rent at 35s a week, payable a quarter in advance

Tommy Bache and Alan Rudkin rescue the sign from the Golden Gloves Amateur Boxing Club's Admiral Street premises after its demolition in 1974. The club, however, did not go out of existence but found a new home in Dingle

They stand,
an oddly matched pair

of bookends on Hope Street,

a street of music, of theatre,
of learning, of entertainment,

a street that affirms the vibrancy
of city life.

They stand to remind us of the other
side of the coin, of our conscience.

In their dwarfing majesty

they remind each of us

that just like each of them,

we are not alone.

Top Stonemasons at work on Liverpool Cathedral in the summer of 1962
Above Let there be light

Light and shade in the crypt of the Metropolitan Cathedral as the Archbishop of Liverpool, Dr Richard Downey,
inspects the newly completed Chapel of the Seven Dolours in 1937

Referee Fred Blakeborough gets a bit too close to the action in this bout between Joe Rufus and Cliff Lawrence at Liverpool Stadium in 1956

It's not the taking part, it's the winning!

Top The Lord Mayor of Liverpool, Frank Cain, kicks off in the Rugby League game between Liverpool City and St Helens at Knotty Ash in October 1957. Predictably Liverpool didn't see too much more of the ball after that, losing 28-4 to Saints

Above Wrapped up against the weather, thousands walk the course on Jump Sunday ahead of the 1951 Grand National

A crowd of 64,318 watch Brian Labone and Ron Yeats lead out the teams for the 1966 Goodison Derby

Top A crowd not quite of Derby Day proportions watch South Liverpool take on Oswestry at Holly Park in 1981

Above Remember your ears buzzing on the way home, remember your face stinging from the ash, remember the smells, hot oil, burning rubber and most of all the sweet smell of methanol, the wood spirit fuel that powered those angry, rasping engines? Remember speedway? Stanley Stadium in 1951

The epic British Grand Prix of 1957. The first world championship race won by a British driver in a British car.
Stirling Moss, in the Vanwall, takes the chequered flag at Aintree